Hello, Zapata! ¡Hola!

By Dr. Ma. Alma G. Pérez

With my best wishes, A. Pérez

Hello, Zapata! ¡Hola!

Published by Del Alma Publications, LLC, Texas
www.delalmapublications.com
Designed by Teresa Estrada & Maricia Rodriguez
Photography by Del Alma Publications, LLC.

ISBN-13 978-0-9822422-1-6
ISBN-10 0-9822422-1-2

Library of Congress Control Number: 2016931029

First Edition

Printed in the United States of America

Dedication

To the children of Zapata County
and of the world,
may you take pride in your communities
and learn as much as you can
about your history, your people, and your places of interest

Dedicatoria

A los niños del Condado de Zapata
y del mundo
ojalá que se enorgullezcan de sus comunidades
y aprendan lo más que puedan
sobre su historia, su gente y sus lugares de interés

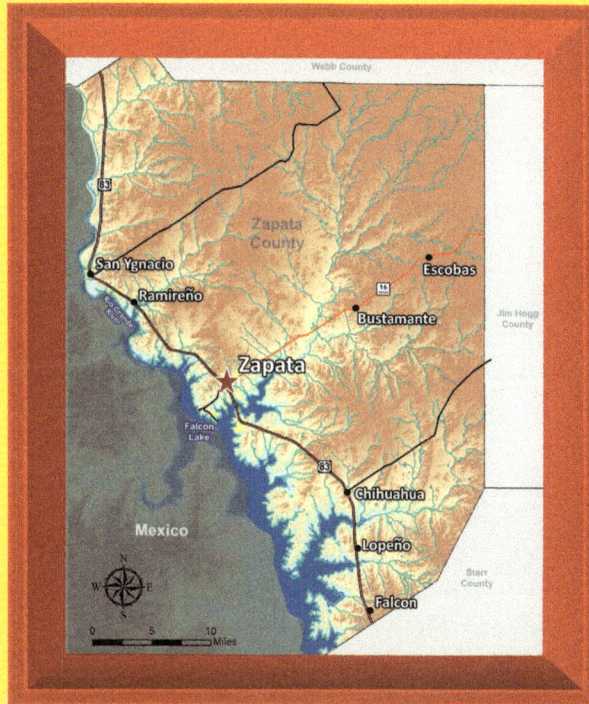

Courtesy of: Victor J. Gonzalez, GISP, CFM, Digidata Technologies, www.DigiDataTech.com

Hello, beloved County of Zapata,
always looking out for your communities
of Zapata, San Ygnacio, Falcón, Lopeño, Chihuahua, Ramireño,
Bustamante, and Escobas as though they were your children.
May we always be proud of our place of origin.

Hola, Condado de Zapata querido,
siempre procurando a tus comunidades
de Zapata, San Ygnacio, Falcón, Lopeño, Chihuahua, Ramireño,
Bustamante y Escobas como si fueran tus hijos.
Ojalá que siempre nos enorgullezcamos de nuestro origen.

Hello, Falcon Dam,
though bringing progress in the midst of tears and sadness,
you keep us connected to our people.
May you always serve as a liaison among ourselves.
Hola, Presa Falcón,
aunque trajiste progreso entre lágrimas y tristeza,
eres el lazo que nos une a nuestra gente.
Ojalá que siempre nos sirvas como eslabón entre nosotros mismos.

Hello, Zapata County Court House,
gracing different views throughout our history,
you have always been the heart of this community.
May you continue to be so.
Hola, Casa de Corte del Condado de Zapata,
luciendo diferentes vistas a través de nuestra historia,
siempre has sido el corazón de esta comunidad.
Ojalá que siempre lo sigas siendo.

Hello, Zapata Town Square,
with your kiosk and your flowers, you add grace to this town.
May your beauty and your splendour always remind us
of the beauty within ourselves.
Hola, Plaza de Zapata,
con tu kiosco y con tus flores, adornas este pueblo con gracia.
Ojalá que tu belleza y tu esplendor nos recuerden siempre
de la belleza dentro de nosotros mismos.

Hello, Zapata County Sheriff's Department,
always ready to serve and to protect,
you provide safety and peace of mind to one and all.
Thank you for taking such good care of us!
Hola, Departamento del Alguacil del Condado de Zapata,
siempre listo para servir y para proteger,
nos ofreces seguridad y confianza a todos y a cada uno.
¡Gracias por cuidarnos con tanto esmero!

Hello, Zapata County Fire Department,
always vigilant, always ready
to render aid wherever you are needed.
We feel safe under your watch.
Hola, Departmento de Bomberos del Condado de Zapata,
siempre vigilante, siempre listo
para asistir donde se necesite.
Nos sentimos seguros bajo tu vigilancia.

Hello, Zapata County Health Center,
serving as a beacon of relief and wellness,
you have calmed the anxiety of many a sick person through the years.
Your presence in this community is greatly appreciated.
Hola, Centro de Salud del Condado de Zapata,
sirviendo como faro de alivio y de bienestar,
has calmado la ansiedad de muchos pacientes a través de los años.
Se agradece mucho tu presencia en esta comunidad.

Hello, Hawk Stadium,
with your bright Friday night lights,
you bring us together to cheer for the mighty Zapata Hawks.
May Hawk Pride transcend generations.
Hola, Estadio Halcón,
con tus luces brillantes de los viernes,
nos reunes para aplaudir a los poderosos Halcones de Zapata.
Ojalá que el orgullo del halcón transcienda generaciones.

Hello, Zapata County Independent School District,
always striving to educate the citizens of tomorrow,
you hold the future of our community and our country in your hands.
May you never lose sight of such a distinct privilege.

Hola, Distrito Escolar del Condado de Zapata,
siempre luchando por educar a los ciudadanos del mañana,
tienes el futuro de esta comunidad y de nuestro país en tus manos.
Ojalá que siempre tengas presente este privilegio tan exclusivo.

Hello, United States Post Office,
rain or shine, as the mail comes through with letters and packages,
you always bring smiles and all kinds of surprises for everyone.
You bring the world to our footsteps.
Hola, Oficina de Correos de los Estados Unidos,
llueva o brille mientras el correo pasa con cartas y paquetes,
siempre traes sonrisas y todo tipo de sorpresas para todos.
Pones al mundo a nuestros pies.

Hello, Arroyo Veleño,
sometimes with water, sometimes without water,
you are always a majestic sight.
May your life extend for generations.
Hola, Arroyo Veleño,
a veces con agua, a veces sin agua,
siempre luces majestuosamente.
Ojalá que tu vida se extienda por generaciones.

Hello, Olga V. Figueroa Public Library,
in the midst of so many books and records,
you remind us of the effort of a truly great woman.
May we all continue to cherish her memory.
Hola, Biblioteca Olga V. Figueroa,
en medio de tantos libros y registros,
nos recuerdas del esfuerzo de una verdadera gran señora.
Ojalá que sigamos venerando su recuerdo.

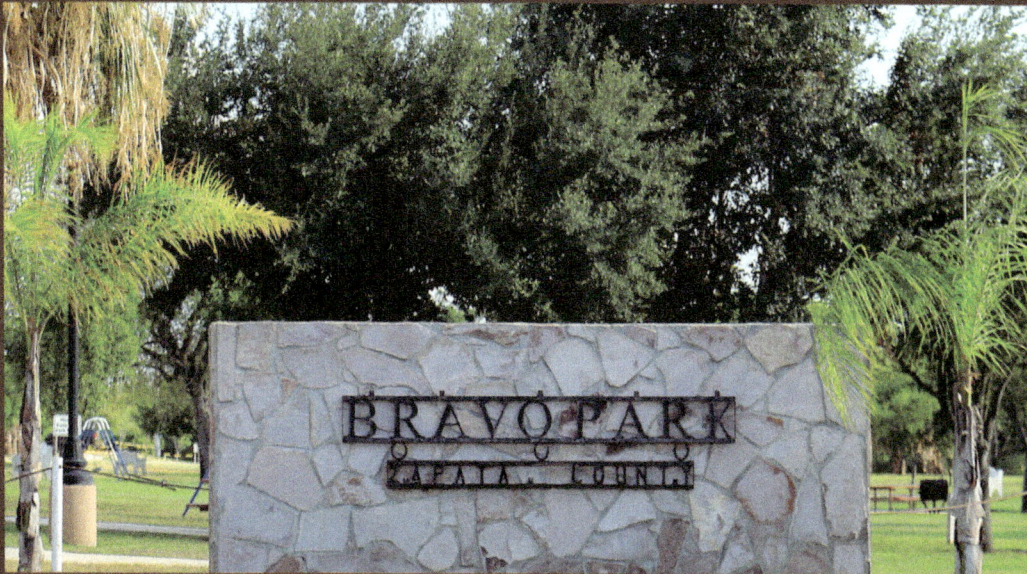

Hello, Bravo Park,
through the cool breeze of spring,
you evoke memories of Judge Manuel B. Bravo.
May his dedication serve as example of commitment to public service.
Hola, Parque Bravo,
mediante la suave brisa de primavera,
evocas recuerdos del Juez Manuel B. Bravo.
Que su dedicación sirva de ejemplo de compromiso al servicio público.

Hello, Zapata County Chamber of Commerce,
always greeting visitors and residents with open arms,
you promote our county and help boost our economy.
You are our window to the world.
Hola, Cámara de Comercio del Condado de Zapata,
siempre recibiendo a huéspedes y a residentes con los brazos abiertos,
promueves nuestro condado y ayudas a fortalecer nuestra economía.
Eres nuestra ventana al mundo.

Hello, famous Falcon Lake,
well known throughout the country,
you are the pride of this community.
May you continue to bring fun times and fond memories to us all.
Hola, famoso lago Falcón,
muy conocido a través de todo el país,
eres el orgullo de esta comunidad.
Ojalá que siempre nos sigas brindando diversión y gratos recuerdos.

Hello, Zapata Technology & Education Center,
you have ushered in a new era for Zapata
as our youth strive for higher academic aspirations.
You will be that tiny seed from which tomorrow grows.
Hola, Centro de Educación y de Tecnología de Zapata,
has traído una nueva época para Zapata
al luchar nuestra juventud por mayores aspiraciones académicas.
Serás esa semillita de donde crezca el mañana.

Hello, Zapata County Museum of History,
depository of our history and of our greatest accomplishments,
you have brought us closer to our ancestors.
May you continue to tell our stories to the children of our children.

Hola, Museo de Historia del Condado de Zapata,
depositorio de nuestra historia y de nuestros más grandes logros,
nos has acercado más a nuestros antepasados.
Que sigas contando nuestras historias a los niños de nuestros niños.

Hello, Plaza Blas María Uribe,
forming the heart and the pride of San Ygnacio,
you evoke memories of the town's founder.
May his memory continue to be honoured by future generations.

Hola, Plaza Blas María Uribe,
formando el corazón y el orgullo de San Ygnacio,
evocas recuerdos del fundador del pueblo.
Ojalá que su memoria siga honrada por las generaciones del futuro.

Hello, Sundial,
our ancestors' way of telling time,
you are a historical marvel and a memorial of the Treviño Fort.
Oh, how wonderful it is to claim you as part of our history!
Hola, Reloj del sol,
el modo de nuestros antepasados de interpretar la hora,
eres una maravilla histórica y un recuerdo del Fuerte Treviño,
Oh, ¡qué maravilloso es reclamarte como parte de nuestra historia!

Hello, La Paz Museum,
a historical jewel, you safeguard a piece of San Ygnacio's history
with great pride and joy.
May you preserve it for years untold.
Hola, Museo La Paz,
una joya histórica, proteges un pedazo de la historia de San Ygnacio
con gran orgullo y con alegría.
Que lo preserves por años sin contar.

Hello, Rio Grande River,
so grand and eternal,
you nourish us with the gift of life.
Never perish in the eternal course of the years.
Hola, Río Grande,
tan grandioso y eterno,
nos alimentas con el don de la vida.
Nunca desvanezcas en el eterno transcurrir de los años.

Hello, Zapata County Community Center,
bringing us together for weddings, quinceañeras
and community events,
you are a symbol of unity for our people.
Hola, Centro Comunitario del Condado de Zapata,
reuniéndonos para bodas, quinceañeras
y eventos de la comunidad,
eres un símbolo de unidad para nuestra gente.

Hello, Intocable Boulevard,
who would have ever thought that the dreams of a young boy
would bring so much glory to this town?
May you always remind future generations of Ricky's brave feat.
Hola, Bulevar Intocable,
¿quién se hubiera imaginado que las aspiraciones de un jovencito
trajeran tanta gloria a este pueblo? Que les recuerdes siempre
a las generaciones del futuro de la valentía de Ricky.

Hello, Guadalupe & Lilia Martínez Swimming Complex,
you are a most popular site in the dog days of summer.
Both young and old
enjoy the soothing feeling of your waters.
Hola, Alberca Guadalupe y Lilia Martínez,
eres un sitio muy popular en los días de canícula.
Tanto los jóvenes como los mayores
disfrutan de la rica sensación de tus aguas.

Hello, Boys & Girls Club of Zapata County,
you provide excellent programs for fun and self development
for the children and youth of Zapata.
Kudos to the sponsors, but especially to the brain behind the idea.
Hola, Club Juvenil del Condado de Zapata,
provees programas excelentes de diversión y desarrollo personal
a los niños y a la juventud de Zapata.
Felicidades a los patrocinadores, pero en especial al genio de la idea.

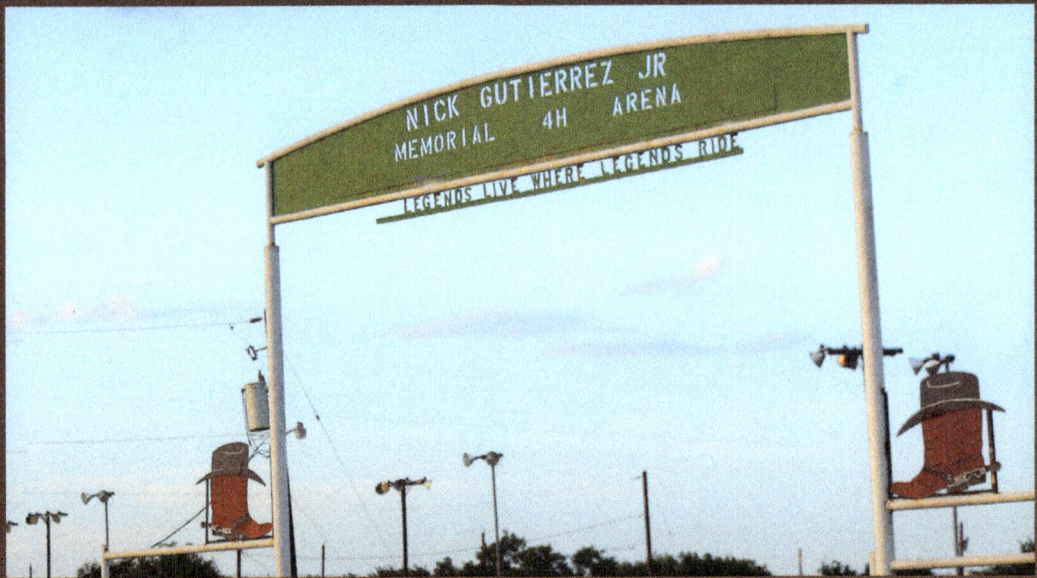

Hello, Nick Gutiérrez, Jr. Memorial 4-H Arena,
rounding up rodeo enthusiasts,
you continue to fill the Gutiérrez family with pride
as the youth of Zapata emulate Nick's special sport.
Hola, Arena Memorial Nick Gutiérrez, Jr.,
reuniendo a entusiastas del rodeo,
sigues llenando de orgullo a la familia Gutiérrez
cuando los jóvenes de Zapata le dan vida al deporte especial de Nick.

Hello, Oswaldo H. & Juanita G. Ramirez Exhibit Hall,
forming the heart of activity every county fair,
you are living proof of the generosity and kind heart
of a truly remarkable couple.

Hola, Salón de Exhibiciones Oswaldo H. & Juanita G. Ramirez,
formando el corazón de actividad cada feria del condado,
eres testamento de la generosidad y noble corazón
de una verdaderamente extraordinaria pareja.

Hello, Zapata County Airport,
Zapata's best kept secret, you connect us to the world
through the foresight and generosity of the Don Abel Ramírez family.
You have brought Zapata County to modern times.
Hola, Aeropuerto del Condado de Zapata,
el secreto más bien guardado de Zapata, nos unes al mundo entero
a través de la anticipación y generosidad
de la familia de Don Abel Ramírez.
Has traído al Condado de Zapata a la época moderna.

Hello, Zapata County Public Boat Ramp,
you have launched many a boat as fishermen from far and near
set out to reel in that coveted prize.
You have greatly boosted the economy of this county.

Hola, Lanzador de Barcas del Condado de Zapata,
has lanzado muchas barcas mientras los pescadores de todas partes
luchan por ese deseado trofeo.
Has fortalecido en gran parte la economía de este condado.

Hello, Falcon State Park,
known for fishing and camping, you represent nature at its best.
May your majestic sunsets and bright summer days
continue to bring joy and fun times to us all.
Hola, Parque Estatal Falcón,
conocido por la pesca y para acampar
representas la naturaleza en su esplendor.
Que tus majestuosos atardeceres y relucientes días de verano
nos sigan trayendo alegría y diversión a todos.

Language Development Activities

Oral Language Development

1. Learn the official place names in English/in Spanish.
2. Share your experiences of field trips with your peers.
3. Bring personal photos of places of interest you have visited.
4. Invite persons in charge of places as guest speakers of the class.

Language Development

1. Learn to spell the official place names in English/in Spanish.
2. Find synonyms for each place name, such as club, plaza, arroyo.
3. Rename place names.
4. Provide brief definitions for key terms: county, boulevard, sundial...

Writing

1. Select your favorite place and research as many facts as possible.
2. Write a description about the important aspects of a particular place.
3. Design a brochure about your favorite place.
4. Make postcards with pictures of places to send to family and friends.

Enrichment/Extension

1. Take field trips to your favorite places of interest.
2. Interview persons in charge of places.
3. Visit similar places of interest in other towns or cities and compare.
4. Research your favorite places of interest.

Vocabulary

airport	club	district	public library
arena	community center	exhibit hall	river
arroyo*	complex	lake	stadium
boat ramp	county	museum	state park
boulevard	court house	park	sundial
center	dam	plaza*	town square
chamber	department	post office	

*Spanish word

Goodbye, Zapata! ¡Adiós!

CPSIA information can be obtained
at www.ICGtesting.com
Printed in the USA
LVOW05s1913260216
476898LV00001B/1/P

9 780982 242216